TROPICAL
QUEENSLAND

![The Skunk Anemone Fish]

The Skunk Anemone Fish of the Great Barrier Reef lives among anemone fronds.

Contents

Cook's Monument was erected in 1887 during Cooktown's ① (see map) boom years and is a tribute to Captain James Cook. (Following pages) Sunset on the Endeavour River at Cooktown.

THE FAR NORTH

At the tip of far northern Queensland lies Cape York, mainland Australia's northern-most point, which is only 150km south of Papua New Guinea. The vast Cape York Peninsula is rugged and largely uninhabited. The first major town down the east coast is Cooktown, over 600km south of the cape. Named after Captain James Cook, the first non-Aboriginal seafarer to explore the east coast, the town is situated at the mouth of the Endeavour River where Cook beached his ship for repairs on that epic journey of 1770. Cooktown was established in 1873 to service the inland goldfields on the Palmer River. During this boom there were 35 000 people, 20 restaurants, 65 pubs and 32 stores. The town has quietened down since then, but today this charming centre stands as a memorial to Cook's accomplishments, and is the access point to Lizard Island, the peninsula and the far northern section of the Great Barrier Reef.

'Cook's Rock' (right), a cairn near the mouth of the Endeavour River, marks the spot where Cook's ship, the Endeavour, *was beached for emergency repairs. Each year in June, Cooktown celebrates this event with its three-day Discovery Festival. The James Cook Museum (below) was originally built as a convent in 1878 and among its exhibits are artefacts from the ship.*

South of Cooktown lie the Cape Tribulation ② and Daintree ③ national parks. Mossman Gorge (left) is a stunning section of the Daintree National Park. At Cape Tribulation (top) the lush verdant rainforest literally meets the sea. All the flora and fauna of the national parks are protected by a World Heritage listing.

The national parks are home to rare birds, terrapins and fruit bats as well as crocodiles (above). Cruise boats (below) leave from the town of Mossman and travel down the Daintree River.

Port Douglas, ④ south of the national parks, also started life as a gold rush port in the 1870s. Today, this small but prosperous resort town at the northern end of Four Mile Beach's sandy crescent is one of the main departure points for Barrier Reef daytrips. Among the onshore attractions is the unique Rainforest Habitat (above).

The Rainforest Habitat (right) has a canopied sanctuary and shelters hundreds of native birds and butterflies, kangaroos (below), emus and freshwater crocodiles.

Stretching your dollar: en route to Cairns, at Smithfield, ⑤ the A.J. Hackett Bungy Company has constructed a giant bungy jumping tower (right) beside the rainforest for the brave souls and the thrill seekers. (Following pages) The Port Douglas Marina Mirage at sunset.

8

CAIRNS AND THE GREAT BARRIER REEF

Cairns, with its international airport and abundance of accommodation, is the unofficial capital of northern Queensland, as well as being a jumping-off point for the northern islands of the Great Barrier Reef, such as Bedarra, Dunk, Fitzroy, Green and Lizard. A variety of excursions departs from here: daytrips to the Barrier Reef, Cape York safaris, whitewater rafting trips and diving courses among others. Cairns' central district has a cosmopolitan mixture of hotels, restaurants and shops, bordered by its wide foreshore esplanade that overlooks Trinity Bay. The bayside hotel and shopping complex known as The Pier is the centre for pleasure craft, charter vessel and ferry departures to the nearby islands and reef. Among all this glamour Cairns still manages to retain the tranquil feel of a relaxed Queensland town. Nestled below the Atherton escarpment, palm trees dot the streets and sugar plantations reside peacefully near the town's edges.

Islands, palm trees and beaches (top) make Cairns ⑥ an idyllic holiday location. Cruise boats (above) depart daily to Green ⑦ and Fitzroy ⑧ islands and the reef from the wharves of the Pier complex. Cairns (right) was initially a gold rush port and later a sugar industry town. Today it is a hub of leisure activities on its twin waterways, Trinity Bay and Trinity Inlet.

The Pier shopping mall in Cairns reflects the city's proximity to the reef with its colourful displays of tropical fish.

The Nutty Choo-choo train is one of the many delights for children of all ages at the Pier shopping mall.

The Tjapukai Aboriginal Dance Theatre (below left) in Kuranda ⑨ presents visitors with local Aboriginal customs; the colourful theatre curtain (left) to the Tjapukai stage.

Kuranda Railway (far left) is one of the most scenically beautiful rail journeys in the world. It links Cairns to Kuranda, the first stop on the Atherton Tableland.

15

The Atherton Tableland (a plateau of the Great Dividing Range which is named after the 1870s pioneer John Atherton) is 'up the hill' from Cairns. Mareeba ⑩ (meaning 'the meeting place of the waters' in local Aboriginal dialect) is inland from Kuranda and the surrounding area is rich with tobacco fields (left).

The average elevation of the Atherton Tableland is 700m; the climate and good soil favour potato and vegetable farming (below), as well as fodder and rice growing. The Tableland also has a 'Waterfall Circuit', the most spectacular cataract being just south of Ravenshoe at the Millstream Falls ⑪ (bottom), which are among the strongest-flowing falls in Australia.

17

The Great Barrier Reef ⑫ (far right) is the largest coral structure in the world. It is home to a variety of fish including this Long-nosed Butterfly Fish (right) and the Harlequin Tusk Fish (bottom).

The Marine Melanesia Crocodile Park (left), on Green Island, has a wonderful collection of Indonesian and Pacific Island artefacts.

Green Island ⑦ is 27km from Cairns. From here, the 'Yellow Submarine' allows a below-the-surface view of the reef without getting wet.

Green Island is a coral cay rather than an island, which means it is formed of sand and coral debris upon which a thick forest has grown; it is surrounded by a fringing reef.

The island was named by Captain Cook in 1770 and is only a one-hour trip from Cairns. (Following pages) The reef comprises some 400 species of colourful coral, which attracts visitors from all over the world.

Townsville ⑬ is some 300km south of Cairns and its wide main streets are notable for well-preserved, late-19th-century architecture such as the Tattersalls Hotel (above) and the historic Queensland Building in the foreground.

Townsville and its harbour (above) can best be appreciated from Castle Hill, which can be reached by foot or by car.

Magnetic Island ⑭ is a short ferry ride from the mainland and is a magnet for visitors who love sailing, waterskiing, swimming and coral viewing. The 5100ha island's shoreline allows the opportunity for a stroll in places like Radical Bay (above and opposite).

Airlie Beach,⑮ the 'front doorstep' to the Whitsunday Islands, has good diving and snorkelling opportunities, while the walking trails of the nearby Conway Range National Park overlook the islands.

THE WHITSUNDAYS AND CAPRICORN COAST

The 74 islands of the Whitsunday Group, just north of Mackay, were named by Captain James Cook in 1770 on the feast of Whit Sunday. Cook was struck by the number of good anchorages, noting that '... the whole passage is one continued safe harbour'. Today the Whitsundays are thronged with yachts, ferries, sea kayaks, and charter boats. Whitsunday Island is the largest – at around 11 000ha – in the Whitsunday cluster known as the Cumberland Islands, where it basks just 13km (and seemingly 1000 years) away from the busy mainland centre of Shute Harbour. Dolphins, parakeets and all other creatures are protected in this superb national park. Its rugged hills are crowned by Mt Whitsunday (435m), but the azure waters and the 6km of Whitehaven Beach's brilliant tidal sands are the island's most famous feature. The waters of this central section of the Great Barrier Reef Marine Park nurture over 1000 species of fish and some 400 species of coral.

Whitehaven Beach (opposite) on Whitsunday Island ⑯ is much the same as when James Cook sailed past. The island is home to goannas, gulls, turtles, and kookaburras, as they share this national park (below) with no one but daytrippers.

Hamilton Island ⑰ seems to have everything, and then some — jet airstrip, huge marina, parasailing, scuba diving, net sports, helicopter picnic excursions to neighbouring islands, and jet skis (above).

Hamilton is distinguished by its high-rise tower and villa accommodation. From its huge freshwater pools (above) to sailing to snorkelling, there's no shortage of ways to get wet and have fun.

Scuba diving and diving lessons are among the most popular activities on Hamilton Island — indeed throughout the Whitsundays.

At 550ha, Hamilton Island is the largest resort complex in the Whitsunday Islands. Its artificial harbour (above and opposite) attracts many sailors and is a transfer hub for surrounding resort islands.

Airlie Beach ⑮ is a superb holiday destination. Restaurants like Magnums (top), good accommodation and the beauty of the Conway Range National Park make it a place to linger. There are plenty of sailing opportunities in everything from yachts to Hobie Cats (centre) or excursion catamarans (left) which enjoy the fair breezes of the beach. Nearby Shute Harbour ⑱ (above) is the main embarkation point for cruises to the Whitsundays. Scuba and snorkelling excursions and island camping can also be arranged here.

Rockhampton ⑲ (top), north of the Tropic of Capricorn, is a thriving service centre for local industry. Lady Musgrave Island ⑳ (right), a tiny, uninhabited coral cay offshore from Bundaberg, is very popular with divers and snorkellers attracted by the excellent coral and fish life of the lagoon. Daytrippers who arrive by the cruise boat Lady Musgrave (above) can also join the underwater activities or cruise the reef in a glass-bottomed boat.
(Following pages) There is nothing more idyllic than when the Lady Musgrave moors on the crystal lagoon waters off its namesake island.

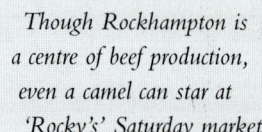

Though Rockhampton is
a centre of beef production,
even a camel can star at
'Rocky's' Saturday markets.

Carnarvon National Park ㉑ is a wonderful oasis inland from Bundaberg. The waters of Carnarvon Creek flow beneath white cliffs of soft sandstone (opposite) at a point known as 'Crossing 18'. The Moss Garden (left) is another of the natural wonders in the park.

There are over 20km of established walking tracks and many ancient Aboriginal rock painting sites throughout Carnarvon National Park, though not all are easily accessible. Among the best known are those in Cathedral Cave (above).

Bundaberg 22 *is a major sugar-growing area. From Hummock Lookout* (above), *the 'green gold' of its bounty creates a beautiful vista and the new cane growth* (below) *can stretch far into the distance.*

Bundaberg is also recognised by its most famous product, 'Bundy' Rum. Within the grounds of the Bundaberg Rum Distillery (bottom and right), *is a museum to show how the rum is made and a pub where it can be sampled.*

Fraser Island ㉓ *is the world's largest sand island and has many contrasts of terrain, from the beautiful Champagne Pools* (top) *to rugged headlands like Waddy Point* (above).

A four-wheel-drive vehicle (far left) *is needed to explore the beaches and inland area of the island. The strangler figs* (left) *and boardwalks of Central Station* (following pages) *are accessible only by foot.*

The Sunshine Coast is abundant in both natural and man-made attractions. There is nothing more tropical than pineapples, and the Big Pineapple (left) at Nambour ㉔ is the best place to sample this tempting fruit.

The Noosa ㉕ coastline is where ocean waves break onto rocky headlands and into sheltered beaches. It is a special place for water sports of all kinds (below) and is backed by coastal vegetation (bottom) with fabulous walking tracks. There are over 70 different colours in the sands at Forty Mile Beach ㉖ (right) which is part of the Noosa Everglades.

BRISBANE AND
THE GOLD COAST

Queensland's sunny state capital sits on the banks of the Brisbane River and has plenty of sophisticated shopping opportunities and good sightseeing. Lone Pine Koala Sanctuary remains one of Brisbane's most popular excursions, while in the mid-city area there are the Botanic Gardens, the 1865 French Renaissance-style Parliament House, the historic stone Post Office (1879) and, harking back to Brisbane's earliest days as a penal colony, the Old Windmill, also known as Observatory Tower (1829) on Wickham Terrace. Australia's third-largest city (of around 1.3 million people) also offers many attractions. Its South Bank complex is a large riverside leisure precinct that encompasses hotels, restaurants, a Maritime Museum, and the Queensland Cultural Centre with its Performing Arts Complex and Gallery. Brisbane also has rich natural hinterlands with rainforest-cloaked mountains and national parks. Within easy reach of the city is the fabulous Gold Coast, full of fun and excitement.

Brisbane's ㉗ river meanders amid great contrasts of scenery, as well as under seven bridges – the most famous being Story Bridge (above) – before it reaches Moreton Bay and the Pacific Ocean. It lends an air of peace to the towering buildings of the central business district (opposite).

One of Australia's most popular tourist spots is the
Gold Coast, a 40km strip of beaches, hotels and
apartments. At its heart is Surfers Paradise ㉘ (left
and top), *famous for its nightlife and sunny beaches.
Theme parks, like Dreamworld (above) and Warner
Bros Movie World, increase the attraction for families.*

*The Gold Coast's most famous event is the Indy Car
Grand Prix in March, but there's plenty to see year-
round like the ship (above) at Sea World.*

From the air, the Great Barrier Reef presents a lacy texture.

First published in 1996 by
New Holland (Publishers) Ltd
London • Cape Town • Sydney • Singapore

Produced in Australia by
New Holland Publishers

3/2 Aquatic Drive, Frenchs Forest
NSW 2086, Australia

80 McKenzie Street, Cape Town 8001
South Africa

24 Nutford Place, London W1H 6DQ
United Kingdom

PHOTOGRAPHIC CREDITS

All photographs New Holland Image Library (Shaen Adey) except for the following: Neville Coleman's Underwater
Geographic Pty Ltd: pp. 18 (Harlequin Tusk Fish), 26 (centre); New Holland Image Library: pp. 34, 35; New Holland
Image Library (Anthony Johnson): pp. 6, 7 (bottom), 12, 13, 15 (top), 18 (second from bottom), 24, 25 (bottom), 26 (top left,
top right, bottom), 27, 45, 48; Ocean Earth Images (Kevin Deacon): pp. 1, 18 (Long-nosed Butterfly Fish), 19, 20–21.

ISBN 1 86436 208 1

Writer: John Borthwick
Designer and typesetter: Alix Gracie
Publishing Manager: Mariëlle Renssen
Commissioning Editor: Sally Bird
Editors: Thea Grobbelaar, Joanne Holliman
Cartographer: John Loubser
Photo Researcher: Vicki Hastrich
Reproduction: Unifoto (Pty) Ltd
Printed and bound in Singapore by: Tien Wah Press (Pte) Ltd